Spark Your Creativity

Unleashing Your Imagination to Ignite a
World of Possibilities

PRADIP N DAS

date, and reliable, complete information. No warranties of any kind are declared or implied. Readers acknowledge that the author is not engaging in the rendering of legal, financial, medical or professional advice. The content within this book has been derived from various sources. Please consult a licensed professional before attempting any techniques outlined in this book.

By reading this document, the reader agrees that under no circumstances is the author responsible for any losses, direct or indirect, which are incurred as a result of the use of information contained within this document, including, but not limited to, — errors, omissions, or inaccuracies.

Table of Contents

Introduction

*"The desire to create is one of the deepest
yearnings of the human soul."
- Dieter F. Uchtdorf*

Four entrepreneurs – Jeff, Elon, Mark, and
Jack – were determined to change the world.
Jeff was a quiet and reserved man with a
passion for books. He started a company that
sold books online and revolutionized the way
people shopped for literature. His company
grew and became known as Amazon. Elon
was a visionary who aimed to make space
travel more accessible to the masses. He
started a company that became known as
SpaceX. Mark was a young and energetic
man who started a social media platform that
connected people from all over the world.
His company became known as Facebook.
Jack was a playful man who loved
technology. He founded a company that

allowed people to send messages in real-time, and his company became known as Twitter.

Together, these four entrepreneurs changed the world by using their creativity and innovative ideas to create companies that touched the lives of millions of people. They inspired others to chase their dreams and showed that with hard work and determination, anything is possible.

Similarly, in a world where technology was king, three tech companies were set out to change the world: Apple, Microsoft, and Google. Steve had a passion for design and aesthetics, and he founded Apple, a company that revolutionized the way people interacted with technology. Bill was a brilliant mathematician who had a vision for a personal computer in every home, and he founded Microsoft. Larry and Sergey together founded a company that changed the way people search for information. Their company, known as Google, became the largest search engine in the world, and they inspired others to chase their dreams and make their ideas a reality.

"Everyone has huge creative capacities. The challenge is to develop them." - Ken Robinson

A team of designers were tasked with creating a new product for a company. They had been brainstorming for days but just couldn't seem to come up with a good idea. They were feeling stuck and frustrated.

One day, one of the team members named Sam decided to take a break from the office and go for a walk. As he was walking, he noticed a group of children playing with sticks and stones. They were having so much fun, and he was struck by the simplicity of their play.

This got him thinking about how people often enjoy simple and natural things, and how they often feel stressed and overwhelmed by technology and the fast-paced nature of modern life. He realized that there was an opportunity to create a product that combined the best of both worlds – a product that was simple, natural, and would help people to de-stress and relax.

Excited by this idea, Sam returned to the office and shared his thoughts with the team. They were all inspired by the idea and quickly got to work on developing a concept. The result was a new kind of smart, minimalist device that was designed to help people unwind and disconnect from the digital world.

The product was a huge success, and the team was proud of what they had created. They had taken a simple observation and turned it into a great idea that made a positive impact on people's lives.

This story shows how a change of perspective and taking a break from the routine can lead to new and creative ideas. Sometimes, inspiration can come from the most unexpected places, and it's important to stay open-minded and have the courage to pursue new opportunities.

Creativity is an ongoing, dynamic process that unfolds throughout a person's life. Here is a fictionalized example of a person's "living story of creativity".

As a child, Mina was constantly scribbling and making art. Her parents enrolled her in art classes and provided her with plenty of materials to work with. Mina felt free to experiment and explored her imagination, and her artistic skills grew rapidly.

"In high school, Mina's art teacher recognized her talent and encouraged her to apply to art school. Mina was accepted and went on to study painting, sculpture, and printmaking. She was exposed to a variety of artistic styles and techniques, and her own work became more focused and sophisticated.

After graduation, Mina worked as a freelance artist, taking on various projects and commissions. She struggled at times to make ends meet, but she never lost her love for making art. Eventually, her reputation grew, and she was offered a job as a visiting professor at a local college.

Over the years, Mina continued to evolve as an artist. She explored new materials and techniques, and her work became more abstract and conceptual. She also became involved in community art projects, working with children and adults to create public art installations.

Now in her 60s, Mina looks back on her life with pride. She feels grateful for the opportunities she's had to express herself creatively and for the people who have supported her along the way. And she knows that her journey with creativity is far from over; there are still new ideas and new forms of expression waiting to be discovered.

Creativity by Accident!

Some creations are made by accident. George Crum, the Native American-African chef at the Moon Lake Lodge resort in Saratoga Springs, New York, is known for inventing the potato chip during his work at the restaurant. He was trying to make fried potatoes, but a customer kept sending them back, asking for them to be thinner and more fried. Although Crum made a thinner batch, the customer was still unsatisfied and insisted on more thinness. Crum finally made fries that were too thin to eat with a fork, hoping to annoy the extremely fussy customer. Surprisingly, the customer loved them, and potato chips were invented!

John Pemberton, the inventor of Coca-Cola, was not a businessman; he was an American pharmacist. He was experimenting with various painkillers and toxins. He blended the base syrup with carbonated water when trying to make another glassful of the beverage, and he got Coca-Cola.

Creativity with Experience!

Creativity is something that one discovers with time, experience, and need. Some are born with it, like prodigies who have overflowing creativity within them. But some take an interest later in their lives, like artists and musicians. Some feel a need to be creative, like writing poems and songs, because they want to express their happiness and sorrow.

Creativity is present in everything, and it's the most profound way in which you can explain your brain and its beauty. Let's say you want to learn guitar. You start learning the basics, and slowly you go deeper into the subject and develop a passion for music. Now you have composed your own original music, which was not possible before because you didn't know anything about it.

Creative ideas pop up when people least expect them. I have also experienced trying to meet a deadline for creative projects. At times when I feel I must be creative to find a solution or meet a deadline, I need to remove myself from the thought process and involve myself in something different. Generally speaking, once I am away from that zone of pressure to produce, ideas seem to flow once again. Every creative person I have ever met has downtimes, and they all have different methods to bring it back. The Muse is always there, yet can be difficult to capture at times.

Creativity when need arises

Creativity often flourishes in times of need when people are faced with a problem that requires a unique solution. This is because the pressure of the situation pushes individuals to think outside the box and come up with innovative ideas that they might not have considered otherwise.

One example of this phenomenon is the story of the legendary British naval leader, Admiral Lord Nelson. In the late 18th century, Nelson was tasked with defeating the French navy during the Napoleonic Wars. He faced a number of challenges, including limited resources and a vastly outnumbered fleet. However, Nelson was not one to back down from a challenge. He used his creativity and resourcefulness to devise a unique battle strategy that would give him the advantage. He ordered his ships to break formation and sail directly at the enemy fleet, a move that was considered daring and unconventional at the time. The strategy worked, and Nelson emerged victorious, solidifying his place as one of the greatest leaders in history.

Another example of creativity in times of need is the story of Wilbur and Orville Wright, the pioneers of human flight. The brothers were passionate about aviation and determined to build a machine that could fly. However, they faced numerous challenges, including limited funding, a lack of understanding of aerodynamics, and general scepticism about the feasibility of powered flight. Despite these obstacles, the Wright brothers continued to experiment and test their designs, using their creativity and problem-solving skills to overcome each challenge. They finally succeeded in building the first successful airplane, launching the age of human flight and inspiring countless others to pursue their own creative dreams.

These stories demonstrate the power of creativity in the face of adversity. When the need arises, people often find the inspiration and determination to come up with innovative solutions, pushing the boundaries of what is possible and making a lasting impact on the world.

Creativity comes from our need to survive and improve the world so it is better for our survival. From art to science, every new product or idea starts with a problem and ends with a solution or expression. There are many kinds of creativity. As humans, we have the ability to feel and remember complex situations. Thus, we can collect our memories, experiences, and learnings and combine them to create something new or altered. In creating something new or altered, we may take a risk but are also often rewarded in the form of praise and/or money. Creativity also often makes a person more interesting, thus more likely to end up with a high-quality spouse or partner, as well as friends who are also creative or interested in solving problems compared to those who accept the world as unchangeable.

In general, creativity stems from our need to have control and cope with life's uncertainty. Whether you are aiming to improve your performance at work or want to live a more fulfilling life, you require a variety of hard and soft skills. One such important skill is critical thinking. A person who practices creativity is often known as a problem solver; people see them as someone who can look at any issue and come up with a great solution. They are able to face challenges more easily, with flexibility and innovative thinking. Creative problem-solving can turn any problem into a solution, no matter what the topic.

Let Your Imagination Fly

"Imagination is everything. It is the preview of life's coming attractions."
- Albert Einstein

Bakul was a young girl living in a small village who had a passion for imagination and creating exciting adventures. Unfortunately, the people in her village did not understand her love for imagination, which caused Bakul to feel discouraged and bored. She found it difficult to be creative and see the world in new and interesting ways. One day, Bakul met a wise old man who was known for his magical stories. He noticed that Bakul was sad and asked her what was wrong. Bakul explained her situation, and the old man gave her a secret: "The power of imagination is like a muscle, it needs to be exercised to stay strong."

The old man taught Bakul how to practice her imagination and see the world in new and different ways. He encouraged her to express her imagination through writing, drawing, or any other creative outlet. With time and practice, Bakul's imagination grew stronger and more vivid, allowing her to turn even the most mundane experiences into exciting adventures. She also began to share her imagination with others, and soon the people in her village began to understand and appreciate her love for creativity. Bakul became a famous storyteller known for her vivid and magical stories, and she continued to exercise her imagination every day, making it an integral part of who she was.

Imagination is a powerful tool that can bring joy and excitement to our lives. By practicing it every day, we can stay creative, innovative, and inspired. Just like young Albert Einstein, who struggled to solve the problem of relativity, but by using his imagination, he was able to solve the theory of relativity. Imagination can help us model ideas and experiment in ways not available to us in reality. Creative imagination can help get us outside of the proverbial box.

Imagination and creativity are closely related and often overlap, with imagination being a key driver of creativity. It allows us to see beyond what is currently in front of us, to picture new possibilities, and envision new ideas. When we use our imagination, we create mental images, scenes, and scenarios in our minds that may not yet exist in the real world. This process of visualizing and exploring new ideas is a crucial step in the creative process and can lead to new insights and innovative solutions.

Artists, writers, scientists, and people in all areas of work use their imagination to explore thoughts in the form of artistic products or innovations. They take different elements already known and re-elaborate them in a new way, making things known in works new to the eye. Imagination provides a foundation for creativity by allowing us to see new possibilities and explore new ideas. By harnessing our imagination and allowing it to inform our creative process, we can tap into our full creative potential and bring new and innovative ideas to life.

What does it take to imagine?

Curiosity is an excellent partner for imagination. When people repeatedly ask "why," "how," and "when," their minds wander, sparking imagination and followed by creativity. By asking oneself questions, trying to understand, asking oneself problems, and then trying to solve them, imagination is exercised, and creativity is fostered.

Imagination creates a short circuit, changes connections, gives space to the impossible, and allows thoughts to flow without being blocked. Exercising the imagination every day of our lives will undoubtedly make us more prepared for creativity. The great thinkers and visionaries of the past started from their imagination, and talent alone would not have taken them far without imagination. Therefore, imagination is the most revolutionary and indispensable act for every human being.

Creating a story by letting one's imagination fly is like doing what is unthinkable. You can do something that you simply cannot do in real life, such as going to the moon and enjoying life there with family. Your story is about what you want to do, with no reality strings attached.

Kids have great imagination power because their minds are a clean slate. For fun, they can come up with the most exquisite drawings and the most innocent and beautiful stories to accompany them. Their thought process is very open and broad.

Let it be understood with the story of Tim. Tim was a very curious and imaginative child who loved to explore the world around him. Despite his young age, he was very creative and always came up with new and exciting ideas.

One day, while exploring the forest near his home, Tim stumbled upon an old, rusty toolbox. He was immediately attracted by it and decided to take it back to his room to see what was inside. To his surprise, he found that the toolbox was filled with all sorts of interesting objects such as hammers, saws, and screws.

Tim's imagination started to run wild as he played with the objects in the toolbox. He began to imagine all sorts of things that he could build with them, like a building or a ship. The more he played with the tools, the more creative he became.

As Tim grew older, he discovered that his imagination was a powerful tool that he could use to help him be more creative. Whenever he was faced with a problem or challenge, he would close his eyes and imagine all the different ways he could solve it. This imagination helped him to think outside of the box and come up with unique and innovative solutions.

Therefore, imagination can be a powerful tool in helping us to be more creative. When we allow ourselves to imagine and dream, we can tap into a world of endless possibilities and come up with ideas and solutions that we never thought were possible.

Creative individuals are more likely than others to possess the personality trait of openness. We can't all be Thomas Edison or Maya Angelou, but creativity is also a state, and anyone can push themselves to be more creative.

Develop Curiosity

"You can't use up creativity. The more you use, the more you have."
- Maya Angelou

Percy Spencer was an engineer and inventor who was working for the Raytheon Corporation in the late 1940s. During a radar project, he observed that the candy bar kept in his pocket had melted. He was curious about why this had happened, and he began to investigate further.

Spencer's curiosity led him to conduct a series of experiments that involved exposing various types of food to high-frequency radio waves. He discovered that the radio waves caused the food to heat up quickly and evenly, leading him to realize that this could be used to cook food much faster than traditional methods. In 1947, Spencer developed the first microwave oven, which revolutionized the way people cook and eat, having a significant impact on modern society.

What is particularly fascinating about Percy Spencer's story is how his curiosity led him to an unexpected discovery. Although he was not searching for a way to cook food faster, his curiosity led him down a path that ultimately resulted in one of the most significant inventions of the 20th century.

Why is curiosity so often linked to success?

Curiosity pushes people towards uncertainty, allowing them to approach it with a positive attitude. Empathy, creativity, innovation, and the ability to learn quickly develop from curiosity.

Curious people welcome surprises in their lives, try new foods, talk to strangers, and ask questions they have never asked before. Genuine curiosity becomes a habit that becomes second nature once you start cultivating it. It seeps into every realm of your life in unexpected ways, from work and friendships to relationships, hobbies, and routines.

Curious people always ask questions and search for answers. Their minds are always active, and since the mind is like a muscle that becomes stronger through continual exercise, the mental exercise caused by curiosity makes your mind stronger and stronger.

Research has shown that epistemic curiosity, when we try to learn new things, activates the reward pathways of dopamine, a neurotransmitter associated with reward in our brains. While some people are naturally curious, curiosity can also be developed.

Curiosity is critical to your success because it signals a hungry mind. If you are inquisitive, you are open to new experiences, generate more original ideas, and produce simple solutions to complex problems.

Curiosity is an essential trait of a genius, and it's hard to find an intellectual giant who is not a curious person. Thomas Edison, Leonardo da Vinci, Albert Einstein, and Richard Feynman are all examples of curious characters, with Feynman being particularly known for his adventures stemming from his curiosity.

In the words of Albert Einstein, "The important thing is not to stop questioning...Never lose a holy curiosity."

Why is curiosity so important?

Curiosity is a driving force behind the process of discovering new ideas and possibilities. When we are curious, we are more likely to question assumptions, challenge conventional wisdom, and explore new paths. Curiosity prompts us to ask questions, seek out information, and explore new perspectives, sparking our imaginations and inspiring us to generate new ideas and possibilities.

Curious people always search for answers in their minds, and their minds are always active. Since the mind is like a muscle that becomes stronger through continual exercise, the mental exercise caused by curiosity makes your mind stronger and stronger.

In addition, curiosity encourages us to see the world in new ways, finding beauty and interest in the unexpected. This inspires us to explore new creative avenues, breaking through creative blocks by encouraging us to take new approaches and explore new directions. It can also help us to see our work in new ways, finding fresh inspiration.

Furthermore, curiosity encourages us to experiment with new techniques and approaches, try new things, and take risks, leading to the discovery of new and innovative solutions.

When you are curious about something, your mind expects and anticipates new ideas related to it. When the ideas come, they will soon be recognized. Without curiosity, the ideas may pass right in front of you, and yet you might miss them because your mind is not prepared to recognize them.

Lastly, the life of curious people is far from boring. Instead of being bored, curious people have an adventurous life, always finding new things to attract their attention and new "toys" to play with.

Children and curiosity

Every child is inherently creative, with an insatiable desire to learn about the world and countless questions filling their minds. Unfortunately, for most people, this natural curiosity diminishes over time. However, curiosity is the starting point for generating ideas, and it is from these ideas that creativity can be sparked. Developing a strong sense of curiosity is therefore essential for both learning and creativity.

As Einstein once said, "Curiosity is more important than intelligence." This means that curiosity is not limited to those who possess high levels of intelligence but rather that it can enhance one's intelligence. Moreover, curiosity is linked to improved engagement and collaboration. Curious individuals tend to make better decisions, perform better, and help their organizations adapt to unpredictable market conditions and external pressures. People who are open and curious orient their lives around a deep appreciation for new experiences and possess an unrelenting drive to explore, discover, and grow. Recent research has even shown that individuals who are open and curious tend to have healthier social outcomes. Therefore, cultivating a strong sense of curiosity can be a powerful tool for unlocking one's creativity and for leading a more fulfilling life.

Children's curiosity is a powerful tool that drives their learning and development. Curiosity is a natural instinct that drives children to explore their environment and ask questions. They are born with an insatiable desire to learn and discover new things. As they grow, their curiosity helps them develop critical thinking skills and a love for learning.

Children's curiosity can be encouraged and nurtured by parents, teachers, and caregivers. They can provide a safe and supportive environment where children can ask questions, make mistakes, and learn through trial and error. Encouraging children's curiosity can lead to a lifelong love of learning and help them develop the skills they need to be successful in school and beyond.

Overall, children's curiosity is a valuable resource that should be cherished and nurtured. It is the foundation of creativity, critical thinking, and problem-solving skills, which are essential for success in all areas of life. By encouraging and supporting children's curiosity, we can help them develop into confident, independent learners who are capable of achieving their goals and dreams.

How to Develop Curiosity

By fostering a spirit of curiosity, we can unlock new creative possibilities and expand our horizons. Curiosity can also be developed and nurtured over time. Here are some strategies that can help you cultivate your curiosity:

Explore new ideas and perspectives: This is essential if you want to have a curious mind.

Be open to learning, unlearning, and relearning. Some of the things you know and believe might be wrong, and you should be prepared to accept this possibility and change your mind. Actively seek out new information and perspectives by reading, watching, and listening to a diverse range of media. This can expose you to new ideas and spark your curiosity. Additionally, engage in activities that are outside of your comfort zone, such as trying a new hobby or visiting a new place. These experiences can expose you to new ideas and perspectives and help you see the world in new ways.

Ask questions relentlessly: One of the simplest ways to develop curiosity is to ask questions. Challenge your assumptions and seek out information by asking questions about the world around you. What is that? Why is it made that way? When was it made? Who invented it? Where does it come from? How does it work? "What," "why," "when," "who," "where," and "how" are the best friends of curious people. As Albert Einstein said, *"The important thing is not to stop questioning. Curiosity has its own reason for existing. One cannot help but be in awe when he contemplates the mysteries of eternity, of life, of the marvellous structure of reality."* Life is full of questions to ask. Live in the present and notice the things that fascinate you most. Solve the mysteries that you can't stop thinking about. When it comes to curiosity, it's the question, not the answer that matters. The journey, however, makes that end result more exciting and satisfying. Curiosity starts the journey and motivates a learner to keep going, no matter how rocky the path.

Make things exciting: Whenever you label something as boring, you close one more door of possibility. Curious people are unlikely to call something boring. Instead, they always see it as a door to an exciting new world. Even if they don't yet have time to explore it, they will leave the door open to be visited another time. You can become more aware of the world around you and more curious about it. Try to focus on your senses, such as what you see, hear, and feel, and pay attention.

See learning as something fun: If you see learning as a burden, there's no way you will want to dig deeper into anything. That will just make the burden heavier. But if you think of learning as something fun, you will naturally want to dig deeper. So look at life through the lens of fun and excitement and enjoy the learning process. Find time to reflect on your experiences and the things that pique your curiosity. Ask yourself why you find certain things interesting and what you can learn from them.

Don't spend too much time in just one world; take a look at other worlds. It will introduce you to the possibilities and excitement of other worlds, which may spark your interest to explore them further. One easy way to do this is through reading diverse kinds of reading. Try to pick a book or magazine on a new subject and let it feed your mind with the excitement of a new world.

Brainstorming

"Brainstorming is like a storm in the brain - a tumultuous, swirling mass of ideas that can lead to great things."
- Colin Mangham

In the 1950s, Toyota struggled to keep up with the demand for their cars, and their manufacturing process was plagued with inefficiencies and errors. To solve this problem, a team of engineers was assembled to come up with a better system.

Initially, the team tried to come up with solutions on their own, but later, they realized that their individual perspectives and experiences were limiting their creativity. Then they decided to try brainstorming as a group, a technique they had heard about from a visiting American consultant.

During the brainstorming sessions, the engineers were encouraged to generate as many ideas as possible, without worrying about whether they were good or bad. They built on each other's ideas, combining and refining them to create better solutions.

Through this process, the team came up with a number of innovative ideas, including the now-famous "just-in-time" manufacturing process. This system enabled Toyota to produce cars more efficiently, with less waste and fewer errors.

The success of Toyota's brainstorming sessions was so significant that it became a fundamental part of the company's culture.

Brainstorming is a powerful technique for generating ideas and promoting creativity. It is a group-based approach that encourages participants to share their ideas and build on each other's contributions. Brainstorming with a group allows for multiple perspectives at the same time, and team members can form new ideas based on each other's suggestions.

Brainstorming is a helpful technique for group projects, especially for teams needing to break out of the same pattern of thinking and develop a new way of viewing something. Engineering teams are usually composed of a diverse mix of individuals, including engineers with expertise in different disciplines, as well as other professionals. Brainstorming allows teams to tap into all the expertise in the group to develop the most successful solution to a design challenge. Some engineering companies specialize in brainstorming unique solutions to design challenges.

Brainstorming encourages participants to generate a large number of ideas without judgment in a short period of time, including both obvious and novel ideas. It encourages a range of viewpoints and ideas that might not have been considered otherwise by bringing together a group of people with diverse backgrounds and perspectives. It can spark creativity by encouraging participants to think beyond their usual constraints and consider new and unexpected ideas. It helps to refine and improve existing concepts, leading to more innovative solutions. It fosters collaboration that promotes teamwork and mutual support, creating a sense of community and fostering a creative and supportive atmosphere.

What are brainstorming techniques?

Brainstorming is a process that enables people to think freely and creatively when trying to come up with ideas, solutions, or sharing knowledge. Brainstorming techniques are proven frameworks for generating lots of ideas quickly. They often include steps to shift perspective, facilitate team collaboration, and refine initial ideas into something even better. You might use proven brainstorming methods to help a group ideate around a problem or new initiative. Some of the core concepts of brainstorming ask that members reserve judgment, go for quality over quantity, listen to all ideas, and think outside of the box in the pursuit of radical new ideas and creative solutions. Brainstorming has been around as long as individuals and teams have tried to find creative and innovative solutions, ideas, or products. Whether a group is ideating on how to solve an organizational problem or generate ideas for new features or initiatives, getting people together to quickly ideate and come up with something new is time well spent.

Classical Brainstorming

Classical Brainstorming is one of the classic brainstorming techniques. Chances are you've done a popcorn brainstorm already. It's been used by everyone to generate ideas and create energy around new initiatives –

much like the popping of corn in a microwave! This is the classic approach to brainstorming, where a group of people comes together and generates as many ideas as possible in a set period of time. Participants are encouraged to build on each other's ideas and defer judgment, and the goal is to generate a large number of ideas. Start by posing a question or problem statement and invite participants to take a minute's silence to think on it. Once the minute is up, start a timer and invite everyone to contribute ideas out loud and build on each other's ideas too. Have a single person take notes and encourage quality over quantity: no evaluation, no criticism or discussion yet – just rapid ideation!

Round-Robin Brainstorming

Round-Robin Brainstorming is a tried and tested idea generation technique that provides a little more structure and ensures everyone in a group can contribute to a brainstorm by ensuring the discussion isn't dominated by the loudest voices. In this group method, seat everyone in a circle and hand them an index card. In silence, everyone writes an idea on their index card before passing it to the person to their left. Each participant then writes an idea based on their neighbour's card and passes that along. The result is a more relaxed session that encourages a combination of idea development and co-creation while ensuring everyone is heard. It's perfect for teams with big personalities!

Mind Mapping

Mind Mapping is a technique that involves creating a visual map of ideas, where each idea is represented as a node on the map. Related ideas are linked together with lines, creating a web of interconnected ideas that can be used to explore different themes and connections. For an organized approach to idea generation, mind mapping is a great activity for creating ideas quickly and effectively. Begin by writing the key topic in the center of a piece of paper or on an online whiteboard. Invite participants to brainstorm related topics and ideas by adding branches to the central idea and creating new nodes or elements. As a facilitator, you'll want to group ideas by color and also adjust the thickness of the branches to show the strength of various ideas and concepts. When you're done, Mind Mapping will result in a diagram that visually represents your group's brainstorming activity and makes it clear how the various ideas interrelate – a great resource for idea development or future sessions!

Rapid Writing

Different teams and workshops need different approaches to generating fresh ideas. While a carefully structured approach can be effective, using quick-fire brainstorming techniques like Rapid Writing can help create a sense of energy, urgency, and get heaps of ideas out quickly. This technique involves having participants write down their ideas on paper rather than sharing them out loud. This can help to level the playing field and ensure that everyone's ideas are given equal weight.

The 5 Whys

It's common to bring underlying assumptions to the brainstorming table when coming up with solutions to problems, which can affect the course of the idea generation process. One way to overcome this challenge is to use The 5 Whys technique, which offers a simple and group-friendly approach to dive further and deeper. To start, collaborate as a group to create a problem statement that you intend to solve. Once you have a clear and concise statement, ask the group why the problem exists and discuss their answers. After achieving a cohesive response, continue to ask the group why the problem exists, repeating the process to unearth the root cause of the issue and move beyond the initial and obvious ideas.

Overall, brainstorming techniques can be a powerful tool for generating ideas and promoting creativity. By providing structure and guidance, these techniques can help to unlock new possibilities and break through creative blocks.

Enhance your Creativity with Criticisms and Feedback

"Criticism is the fertilizer that helps creativity grow." - Joel Garreau

Lily had a great passion for painting and used to paint every day, with her paintings being appreciated by her friends and family. One day, Lily decided to participate in a local art competition in the hopes of gaining recognition for her talent. When the day of the competition arrived, Lily was excited and confident, having put a lot of effort into her painting. However, she was shocked when the judges announced that her painting was not among the winners. Feeling disappointed and discouraged, Lily considered giving up on her passion for painting.

On her way home, Lily remembered a quote she had read, "Criticism is a chance to grow." She realized that the judges' comments were not meant to discourage her but to help her improve. Instead of giving up, she decided to take the criticism constructively and use it to become a better painter. Lily returned to her studio and used the judges' comments as a guide to improve her skills. With time and effort, Lily became a professional painter who received recognition and praise for her works.

Criticism is not something to fear, but something to embrace. If we use it to our advantage, it can help us become better versions of ourselves and achieve great things. Therefore, the next time you face criticism, take it positively and use it to grow and improve. Analyze criticism to find something you can learn from it, whether it be at work, school, or social clubs. We all make mistakes, and learning how to deal with criticism positively is one way to improve our interpersonal relationships with others.

J.K. Rowling faced numerous rejections from publishers when trying to get her manuscript for Harry Potter and the Philosopher's Stone published. She was rejected by twelve different publishers before being accepted by Bloomsbury. Even after finding a publisher, Rowling continued to receive criticism and negative feedback on her writing. However, she used the feedback to fuel her creativity and improve her writing. The result was a series of books that have become some of the best-selling and most beloved novels of all time.

Dealing with criticism positively is an important life skill. At some point, you will face criticism, and sometimes it will be difficult to accept. You can either use criticism positively to improve or negatively to lower your self-esteem and cause stress, anger, or even aggression. Therefore, it's important to use criticism constructively to grow and become a better version of yourself.

How to Convert Criticism into Creativity

Converting criticism into creativity can be a challenging process, but it is possible with the right mindset and approach. Here are some tips on how to turn criticism into a source of creative inspiration:

- *Don't take it personally:* When we receive criticism, it can be easy to take it personally and become defensive. However, it is important to remember that criticism is not a personal attack, but rather an opportunity for growth and improvement.

- *Listen actively:* When someone is giving you feedback or criticism, listen actively and try to understand their perspective. Ask questions and clarify their points to ensure you fully understand their feedback.

- *Look for the nuggets of truth:* Even if the criticism is harsh or difficult to hear, there may be some truth to it. Look for the nuggets of truth in the criticism and use them to improve your work.

- *Reframe the criticism:* Instead of seeing criticism as a negative, try to reframe it as a positive. View it as an opportunity to learn and grow, and as a source of creative inspiration.

- *Experiment and try new things:* Use the criticism as a starting point for experimentation and trying new approaches. Explore different ways of approaching the problem or challenge, and use the feedback to inform your creative process.

- *Practice resilience:* Converting criticism into creativity requires resilience and perseverance. Keep working on your creative projects, even if the criticism is difficult to hear. Use the criticism as motivation to keep improving and growing as a creative person.

By adopting these approaches, you can turn criticism into a source of creative inspiration and use it to improve your work and grow as a creative person.

Challenge, Creativity and Success

"Challenges are what make life interesting, and overcoming them is what makes life meaningful." - Joshua J. Marine

Prag, who lived a very comfortable life, had a good job, a nice house, and plenty of money, but he was not happy. He felt like his life was monotonous and lacked excitement.

One day, Prag came across a quote that said, "Challenge yourself every day to become a better person." He realized that the reason he was unhappy was that he had not been challenging himself enough. He was stuck in his comfort zone and had not been pushing himself to grow and improve.

From that day on, Prag decided to challenge himself every day. He started with small challenges, like trying a new food or learning a new skill, and gradually worked his way up to bigger challenges, like hiking a mountain or learning a new language.

With each new challenge, Prag began to feel more confident and alive. He discovered a sense of purpose and joy in life that he had not felt before. He became more creative and innovative, and his life was filled with new experiences and exciting adventures.

Years went by, and Prag had become a completely different person. He was no longer stuck in his comfort zone, but was always pushing himself to be better and do better. He had become an inspiration to others, who saw in him the power of challenging oneself to achieve great things.

Therefore, challenging ourselves every day can help us break out of our comfort zones and become better versions of ourselves. Whether it's a small challenge or a big one, pushing ourselves to do something new and different can help us grow, improve, and lead a more fulfilling life.

In everyday life, there are ample opportunities to challenge yourself. Changing your work style can also encourage you to think about your routines differently. You could change the way you perform a certain task or learn more about a different department each day.

The challenge is to do something different every day and observe. It may be practicing meditation in the morning, turning off your smartphone during work, switching off the television while having dinner, starting to read books, or going for a walk for an hour. These changes can break you out of old, comfortable routines.

How Challenges develop creativity

Rimi had always been fascinated by the beauty of nature and was passionate about capturing it in her art. She would spend hours painting the colorful flowers in her garden, the rolling hills in the distance, and the bustling wildlife that surrounded her.

However, despite her love for art, Rimi found that she was becoming increasingly stuck in a creative rut. She found herself using the same techniques and materials over and over again, and her paintings were starting to look the same. She was feeling uninspired and lacked the passion she once had for her craft.

One day, while wandering through the village, Rimi met an old artist named Richard. Richard was known throughout the village as the most creative artist of all time. He had a reputation for pushing the boundaries of what was possible with art and coming up with innovative new techniques.

Rimi was inspired by Richard and asked him for advice on how she could become more creative in her own work. Richard replied,

"Creativity comes from facing challenges and overcoming them. You must push yourself out of your comfort zone and try new things."

And so, Rimi decided to take Richard's advice. She set herself a challenge to create a series of paintings using only materials that she had never used before. This was a huge challenge for Rimi, who was used to using only traditional materials such as oil paints and canvases.

However, as she worked on her paintings, Rimi found that the new materials sparked a new level of creativity in her. She discovered new ways of expressing herself, and her work became more vivid and dynamic. Her paintings were now filled with life and energy, and she was feeling more passionate about her art than ever before.

From that day forward, Rimi continued to set herself new challenges and explore new materials and techniques. She became known throughout the village as the most innovative and creative artist of all time. And so, the story of Rimi and her challenges shows us that challenges can be a powerful tool in helping us to be more creative. By pushing ourselves out of our comfort zones and trying new things, we can tap into a world of new possibilities and bring our creativity to new heights.

Challenges are often seen as obstacles to be overcome, but they can also be opportunities to develop creativity and innovation. Here are a few ways that challenges can improve creativity for successful people:

- *Forces you to think outside the box:* When faced with a challenge, successful people must find creative solutions that go beyond the obvious or traditional approaches. This requires them to think outside the box and find new and innovative ways to tackle the problem.

- *Fosters a growth mindset:* Challenges can help successful people develop a growth mindset, where they view obstacles as opportunities to learn and grow. This can encourage them to take risks and push themselves beyond their comfort zone, leading to new ideas and innovations.

- *Encourages experimentation:* When faced with a challenge, successful people may need to experiment with different approaches and solutions to find the most effective solution. This can lead to new ideas and approaches that might not have been considered otherwise.

- *Builds resilience:* Overcoming challenges can build resilience, which is an essential trait for creative and successful people. By persevering in the face of adversity, successful people can develop the strength and determination needed to push through creative blocks and find new solutions.

- *Promotes collaboration:* Challenges can also encourage successful people to collaborate with others, bringing together different perspectives and ideas to find the best solution. This can lead to more creative and innovative ideas than working alone.

In general, obstacles have the potential to be a valuable resource in enhancing creativity and innovation for accomplished individuals. By stimulating them to explore unconventional ideas, nurture a mindset of development, take risks, develop durability, and work in partnership with others, obstacles can result in novel and inventive resolutions that enable them to accomplish their objectives.

Creativity and Success

Successful entrepreneurs often face setbacks and failures on their path to building their careers or businesses. By viewing these setbacks as opportunities to learn and grow, they develop new ideas and strategies that ultimately lead to success. They constantly adapt to new technologies and changes in their industries, which encourages them to experiment with new ideas and find innovative solutions to problems.

Successful artists and writers often face creative blocks and challenges when developing new work. They view these challenges as opportunities to experiment and try new things, and they find new sources of inspiration to develop innovative new works.

In many fields, such as engineering and science, professionals work on complex problems that require innovative solutions. By collaborating with others and thinking creatively, successful professionals find new and innovative ways to solve these problems.

When faced with the challenge of developing a new product, successful companies think outside the box and find new and innovative ways to meet customer needs. Here are some examples of successful people who have used challenges to improve their creativity:

One of my favorites is Tony Robbins, a motivational speaker, and life coach who has helped millions of people achieve their goals. He has faced numerous challenges throughout his life, including a difficult childhood and financial struggles. He has developed innovative techniques for personal development and empowerment that have transformed the lives of people around the world.

J.K. Rowling is a writer who faced many challenges while writing the Harry Potter series, from rejection by multiple publishers to personal struggles with depression. By persevering through these challenges and using her imagination and creativity, she created a beloved series of books that has inspired millions of readers around the world.

Malala Yousafzai is an activist for education and women's rights who survived an assassination attempt by the Taliban in Pakistan. She has continued to speak out for the rights of girls and women around the world, using her creativity and resilience to inspire change and make a positive impact.

Serena Williams is one of the greatest tennis players of all time, with over 20 Grand Slam singles titles to her name. She has faced many challenges throughout her career, including injuries and intense competition. By using her creativity and determination, she has developed a unique playing style that sets her apart from her competitors and has inspired a generation of tennis players.

Simone Biles is an Olympic gymnast who has faced several challenges throughout her career, including injuries and the pressure of competing at the highest level. But, she has developed new and innovative techniques that have set her apart from her competitors, making her one of the most successful gymnasts of all time.

These are just a few examples of successful people who have used challenges to improve their creativity and achieve their goals. Challenges can be a powerful driver of creativity and innovation for success.

Ask Question

"The power to question is the basis of all human progress." - Indira Gandhi

Sophia was feeling stuck in her creative process. No matter how hard she tried, she just couldn't come up with any new ideas for her artwork. Frustrated, she decided to take a walk in the park to clear her head.

As she strolled through the park, she noticed a group of children playing and asking each other questions. Suddenly, it dawned on her that perhaps the key to unlocking her creativity was simply to start asking more questions.

When she returned home, Sophia decided to try an experiment. She would spend the next week asking as many questions as she could about the world around her. Every day, she would ask her family, friends, and even strangers about their experiences and perspectives.

To her surprise, this exercise in questioning led to a surge in creativity. She discovered new ideas and insights she never would have thought of on her own. Her conversations with others opened up new avenues of thought and helped her make connections between things she had never seen as related before.

By the end of the week, Sophia had filled several notebooks with ideas for new art pieces. She went to her studio with renewed energy and created some of her best work yet.

From that day forward, Sophia continued to ask questions as a regular part of her creative process. By doing so, she was able to tap into new sources of inspiration and continuously push the boundaries of her artistic abilities.

Asking questions is a powerful tool that can stimulate creativity and imagination. When we ask questions, we force ourselves to think outside the box, to look at things from different angles, and to consider alternative solutions and perspectives. This opens up new avenues for creative thought and allows us to see things in new and innovative ways.

Asking questions also helps us gather information and learn about new concepts and ideas, which can spark new thoughts and ideas of our own. By questioning the status quo and challenging conventional wisdom, we can come up with unique and original ideas that might not have been considered otherwise.

Furthermore, asking questions can lead to collaboration and the exchange of ideas with others. When we ask questions, it can lead to improved creativity by fostering new perspectives, challenging assumptions, and inspiring new ideas.

My teacher used to say that when we do not find a solution to any problem, we should ask questions instead of seeking an answer. Instead of looking for new answers, consider changing the types of questions you ask. Brainstorm a list of open-ended questions to ask when addressing a common challenge. Good questions will help you think about your processes and how you might be able to change them to improve your productivity.

When you ask a question, you start working from a different perspective, and you can improve your creative-thinking skills. While you may have to consciously consider thoughts and solutions from alternative perspectives, you may find that the process becomes easier over time.

Questions can lead you to more creative insight due to directing your thinking in a way that requires an answer. Your brain is a goal-seeking mechanism, so by asking questions, you prompt it to find an answer. These questions can provide a way of looking at a problem that provides solutions you hadn't thought about before.

When a problem surfaces, it is very easy to stay within a problem state. Constantly looking at the problem doesn't necessarily provide a solution. By turning the problem into a question, you are directing your thinking towards finding a solution.

An example of this would be "I need more money". This is the problem, but to start generating a solution you need to ask questions, such as "Who do I know that could help me to earn more money?" to direct your thinking.

The moment a question pops up, our brain gets to work instantly. Questions create a whole world of new discoveries and creative insights. Questions are like fuel for your brain, and when used regularly, they can skyrocket your success. Human beings are hard-wired to generate answers and dig for possible solutions. That's why asking questions is such a powerful tool and an essential skill for every creative problem solver. Learn to ask better questions, and you will get better ideas.

I find that one of the best ways to spark creativity is by sitting quietly and creating a list of 100 questions. There is no direction as to what questions to ask. Once you start asking questions, they take on an entirely different tone, and learning focuses more on what you want to discover. It creates a miracle in terms of going deep and creating options. Questions give us focus and direction, and keep tricking our head to find answers.

Questioning can solve many problems automatically by activating the lethargic mind. Even if it couldn't solve the problem, it reminds our mind repeatedly to find solutions. So the habit of questioning should be practiced so that creativity develops, which helps us to grow.

Needless to say, some of the questions above lead to new ideas for sales, while others will simply help you discover interesting insights on how to improve your existing business.

How Asking Questions Stimulate Creativity?

In the early 1980s, Steve Jobs was developing the first Macintosh computer. He was determined to create a computer that was not only functional, but also beautiful and easy to use. To achieve this, he asked his team a simple but powerful question: "What would happen if we made the computer friendly?"

This question sparked a creative process that led to the development of the first graphical user interface (GUI) for a computer. The GUI made the Macintosh computer easy to use, even for people who had no experience with computers.

Jobs' willingness to ask questions and challenge the status quo was a key driver of his creativity. He believed that by asking questions and pushing the limits of what was possible, he could create products that would change the world.

The development of the first Macintosh computer is just one example of how asking questions can lead to creative breakthroughs. By asking the right questions and challenging assumptions, we can unlock new insights and perspectives that can lead to innovative solutions.

Asking questions can stimulate creativity in a number of ways. Let's say you work in the dairy industry and are looking to develop a new product that will appeal to a wider range of consumers. Instead of relying on the same old ideas, you decide to ask yourself some questions to stimulate your creativity and generate new ideas.

First, you might ask yourself some broad questions like: "What are the current trends in the dairy industry?" or "What are some common consumer complaints or desires when it comes to dairy products?" These questions can help you identify potential areas of opportunity or improvement that you may not have considered before.

Then, you might start asking more specific questions like: "What are some unique flavor combinations that we could try in our dairy products?" or "How can we make our products more convenient for on-the-go consumption?" These questions can help you brainstorm new and innovative ideas that differentiate your product from competitors and cater to the needs and desires of your target consumers.

As you continue asking questions, you may also consider more unconventional ideas, such as: "What if we created a plant-based dairy product to cater to the growing demand for plant-based options?" or "How can we use technology to improve the production and distribution of our products?" These kinds of questions can help you generate truly innovative ideas that push the boundaries of traditional dairy products and set your company apart in the market.

By asking questions and exploring different possibilities, you can unlock your creativity and generate fresh ideas that can lead to exciting new products and growth opportunities in the dairy industry.

In short, asking questions helps to stimulate creative thinking by encouraging divergent thinking, expanding knowledge, sparking new connections, challenging assumptions, and facilitating collaboration.

Believe The Impossible

"The only limit to our realization of tomorrow will be our doubts of today. Let us move forward with strong and active faith." - Franklin D. Roosevelt

Mia, who lived in a small village, was born with a love for art. From a young age, she had a natural talent for painting and drawing. However, despite her abilities, Mia never believed in herself. She always thought that her work was never good enough and that she could never be as good as the other artists in her village.

Mia's self-doubt held her back, and she stopped pursuing her love for art. She convinced herself that she was not cut out to be an artist, and her work would never be good enough.

One day, a famous artist came to Mia's village and held a workshop. Mia decided to attend, and as she worked alongside the other artists, she was amazed at how talented they all were. She realized that everyone had their own unique style, and there was no such thing as a "perfect" artist.

During the workshop, the famous artist noticed Mia's talent and offered to mentor her. He showed her that true creativity comes from within and that the only thing holding her back was her self-doubt. He taught her that the key to unlocking her creativity was to believe in herself and her abilities.

Mia took the artist's words to heart and started to believe in herself. She started to create again, and to her surprise, her work was better than ever. She found that her self-doubt had been blocking her creativity, and by believing in herself, she was able to tap into a whole new level of creativity that she had never experienced before.

Mia's work caught the attention of the other artists in the village, and she soon became known as one of the most talented and creative artists in the region. The story of Mia shows us that believing in ourselves is essential to unlocking our creativity. When we believe in ourselves, we can tap into our full potential and create things that we never thought were possible.

Believing in the impossible can help expand your creative thinking and open up new possibilities for innovation and discovery. It allows you to approach problems and challenges from a new perspective, leading to fresh and unique solutions.

When you believe in the impossible, you are forced to think beyond what is currently feasible or logical. This encourages you to think creatively and consider unconventional solutions that may not have been considered otherwise.

Believing in the impossible allows you to tap into your imagination and think beyond what you have experienced or know to be true. This can lead to the creation of entirely new ideas or concepts.

Believing in the impossible can help you overcome mental barriers that may be holding you back from achieving your creative potential. By breaking down these barriers, you can think more freely and creatively.

When you believe in the impossible, you are more likely to take risks and try new things. This can lead to breakthroughs and new discoveries that you may not have achieved otherwise.

When Musk founded SpaceX in 2002, his goal was to make space travel more affordable and accessible by developing reusable rockets. At the time, the idea of reusable rockets was considered impossible by many experts in the field, as no one had been able to successfully achieve it.

Despite the skepticism and numerous setbacks along the way, Musk and his team persisted in their efforts to make reusable rockets a reality. They experimented with new technologies and techniques, learning from their failures and making incremental progress with each attempt.

In 2015, SpaceX achieved a major milestone when they successfully landed a reusable rocket for the first time. This breakthrough not only proved that reusable rockets were possible but also marked a significant step forward in the quest to make space travel more sustainable and affordable.

Through their perseverance and willingness to believe in the impossible, Musk and his team were able to push the boundaries of what was considered possible and achieve a breakthrough that has revolutionized the aerospace industry.

This is a powerful example of how believing in the impossible can inspire creativity and lead to innovative solutions that transform our world.

Nelson Mandela was a South African anti-apartheid revolutionary and political leader who believed that the end of apartheid in South Africa was possible, even when many people thought it was impossible. He spent 27 years in prison for his efforts to end apartheid, but he never lost faith in the possibility of a free, democratic South Africa. His perseverance and leadership led to the eventual end of apartheid and the establishment of a democratic government in South Africa.

The Wright Brothers are famous for their invention of the first successful powered airplane. At the time, many experts believed that human flight was impossible. However, the Wright Brothers persisted and through their creativity and experimentation, they were able to achieve what many thought was impossible.

The Internet is a global network of interconnected computers that has transformed the way we communicate, do business, and access information. When it was first developed in the 1960s, many experts believed that a network of interconnected computers was impossible. However, a group of researchers and engineers believed in the impossible and were able to create a system that has since revolutionized the world.

When Apple first introduced the iPhone in 2007, it was a device that revolutionized the smartphone industry. At the time, many experts believed that it was impossible to create a device that combined a phone, camera, and media player in one package.

However, Apple's designers and engineers believed in the impossible and were able to create a product that has since transformed the way we communicate and consume media.

Penicillin is a life-saving antibiotic that has saved millions of lives. It was discovered by Sir Alexander Fleming in 1928, after he noticed that a mold growing on a petri dish was killing the bacteria around it. At the time, many experts believed that antibiotics were impossible, but Fleming believed in the impossible and his discovery revolutionized medicine and has since been used to treat a wide variety of illnesses and infections.

Electric cars have been around for over a century, but it wasn't until recently that they became a viable alternative to traditional gas-powered cars. For a long time, many experts believed that electric cars were impractical and would never catch on. However, a group of designers, engineers, and entrepreneurs believed in the impossible and developed new battery technology, charging infrastructure, and business models that have helped to make electric cars a viable and popular alternative to gas-powered cars.

Solar energy is the technology that allows us to capture the sun's energy and use it to power our homes and businesses. At the time of its invention, many experts believed that solar energy was impractical and too expensive to be a viable alternative to traditional energy sources. However, a group of engineers, designers, and entrepreneurs believed in the impossible and developed new solar technologies, materials, and financing models that have helped to make solar energy a competitive and popular alternative to fossil fuels.

Virtual reality is a technology that allows us to experience immersive, computer-generated environments. At the time of its invention, many experts believed that virtual reality was impossible due to technical limitations and the high cost of the equipment needed. However, a group of researchers and engineers believed in the impossible and developed new VR technologies, hardware, and software that have made virtual reality a popular and accessible technology for a wide range of applications, from gaming to education.

Space tourism is the concept of allowing private citizens to travel to space for recreational purposes. At the time of its conception, many experts believed that space tourism was impossible due to the high cost, technical complexity, and safety concerns involved. However, a group of entrepreneurs and engineers believed in the impossible and developed new space technologies, launch systems, and spacecraft that have made space tourism a reality.

Autonomous vehicles are self-driving cars that use sensors and artificial intelligence to navigate roads and traffic. At the time of their conception, many experts believed that autonomous vehicles were impossible due to the technical complexity and safety concerns involved. However, a group of engineers, researchers, and entrepreneurs believed in the impossible and developed new autonomous vehicle technologies, algorithms, and testing methods that have helped to make self-driving cars a reality.

These examples show how believing in the impossible can inspire creativity and lead to innovative solutions that have the potential to transform our world. By challenging assumptions and thinking creatively, we can achieve breakthroughs that have the potential to improve our lives and create a better future.

If we believe in the impossible and are willing to work hard to achieve it, we can accomplish great things. Our beliefs have the power to shape our lives, and by believing in ourselves and our abilities, we can turn our dreams into reality. So, believe in the impossible, and see what you can achieve!

Learn By Doing

"Tell me and I forget, teach me and I may remember, involve me and I learn."
- Benjamin Franklin

Learning is a natural process. It comes from experiences, thought processes, learning abilities, habits, imagination, and training our subconscious mind, among other things. A young man named Jack wanted to become a chef. He had a passion for cooking and had always loved experimenting with new recipes and ingredients. However, despite his love for cooking, Jack struggled to make it as a chef.

One day, Jack decided that he needed to take his education to the next level. He knew that simply reading cookbooks and watching cooking shows wasn't enough - he needed to actually get in the kitchen and start cooking.

So, Jack enrolled in a cooking course at a local community college.

At first, Jack was intimidated by the kitchen. He was used to cooking at home, but the professional kitchen was a completely different environment. However, he soon learned that the best way to improve was by doing. He got his hands dirty and started experimenting with new recipes and techniques.

Jack quickly discovered that the experience of cooking was much different than just reading about it in a book. He was able to learn by doing and gain valuable hands-on experience that he couldn't have gotten any other way. He learned how to properly chop vegetables, how to properly season food, and how to plate dishes in a way that was both aesthetically pleasing and delicious.

By the end of the cooking course, Jack felt confident in his abilities as a chef. He applied for a job at a local restaurant and was soon hired as a line cook. Over time, Jack continued to improve and grow as a chef, and eventually, he was promoted to head chef.

Therefore, learning by doing can be a powerful tool for growth and development. By immersing yourself in a new experience and actively engaging with it, you can gain knowledge and skills that simply can't be gained from reading or watching. So, if you have a passion for something, don't be afraid to jump in and start learning by doing.

Richard Branson, the founder of Virgin Group, started his first business venture at the age of 16, when he launched a magazine called Student. He learned a lot from this venture, such as marketing, advertising, and the importance of networking.

However, it was his next venture that truly showcased the power of learning by doing. In 1972, Branson started a mail-order record business, which he named Virgin Records. At the time, Branson knew nothing about the music industry, but he was passionate about music and believed that he could learn as he went along.

He started by placing ads in music magazines and receiving orders through the mail. He then started selling records through a stall in Oxford Street, London. Branson learned about the music industry by listening to the records he was selling and talking to customers. He discovered that there was a demand for underground and alternative music, which was not being met by the major record labels.

Through trial and error, Branson built up his business and eventually opened his record store. He signed his first artist, Mike Oldfield, who recorded the hit album "Tubular Bells" for Virgin Records. Branson then expanded his business by starting a record label and signing other artists.

Branson's success with Virgin Records was not just due to his passion for music but also his willingness to learn by doing. He learned about the music industry by taking risks and trying new things. He made mistakes along the way, but he used them as learning opportunities.

Today, the Virgin Group is a multinational conglomerate with over 400 companies in various industries, including travel, entertainment, and telecommunications. Branson's success can be attributed to his entrepreneurial spirit and his willingness to learn by doing.

Elon Musk has always been a self-learner, teaching himself how to code at the age of 12 and creating his own video game shortly after. One of Musk's early entrepreneurial ventures was Zip2, a company he co-founded in 1995 that provided business directories and maps to newspapers. Musk had no formal education in computer science or business, but he taught himself how to program and built the software platform for Zip2 himself.

Musk's willingness to learn by doing also played a key role in the development of SpaceX, his private space exploration company. When Musk founded SpaceX in 2002, he had no experience in the aerospace industry. He learned about rockets and space exploration by reading books, talking to experts, and most importantly, building and launching rockets himself. Musk's team encountered many setbacks and failures along the way, but they used these experiences as opportunities to learn and improve their designs.

Similarly, Musk's approach to developing electric cars at Tesla involved a lot of learning by doing. He pushed the boundaries of traditional automotive engineering and manufacturing by developing new technology and methods. Musk was involved in every aspect of Tesla's product development, from designing the batteries to developing the software. Through his hands-on approach, Musk was able to develop electric cars that could compete with traditional gasoline-powered vehicles in terms of performance, range, and convenience.

These examples demonstrate the power of learning by doing. Successful entrepreneurs like Branson and Musk were not afraid to take risks, try new things, and learn as they went along. They embraced failure as a necessary part of the learning process and used their experiences to innovate and create successful businesses.

In general, we do not learn many things in school. We learn while living our lives, actually by doing, not by just reading or listening about doing. Confucius once said, "I hear, I forget. I see, I remember. I do, I understand."

Reading Improves Creativity

"Reading is a way for me to expand my mind, open my eyes, and fill up my heart."
- Oprah Winfrey

There was a mighty king who lived in a luxurious palace mounted at the top of a mountain. The king had a mighty army of around 20,000 soldiers protecting the fort. I am sure that while reading this fictitious story, you had vivid pictures created in your mind. As it has been said, imagination is a tool for creativity. We can only read when we imagine the things being written. This is how reading makes you imaginative, leading to creativity.

Our brain is like a super-powerful advanced computer, and like all good computers, the better the information in, the better the information out. Like all good computers, your mind needs good information for good output. Reading is the best source of inputs you can feed the brain. You need to nourish your brain with new and good information. Without new information, the mind becomes stagnant. Reading feeds your hungry mind with an endless supply of knowledge and information which it seeks. Reading can help broaden your mind or keep you intrigued in a storyline where the power of curiosity will make you want to get to the end of the book as quickly as possible.

Reading increases your imagination and creativity. It also gives you different ideas and understanding. A good reader from a young age can become a good writer. Reading sparks one's imagination. When you read, you are taken into a new world. The content nurtures your brain to develop ideas for new worlds and other possibilities, which sparks the imagination. Reading helps you to understand differently.

Reading exposes you to the world of imagination; it shows you that nothing is impossible in this world, and it shows how different actions lead to different results. Books help you change your fixed mindset to a growth mindset.

Research says that the brain requires exercise to keep it strong and healthy. Hence, reading can be the best exercise to keep your brain healthy, fit, and strong. Similarly, games like chess, puzzles, analytical reasoning, etc., can also stimulate the brain. Great books have been written by some of the best and most creative minds. By reading those books, you can delve into what goes on in the inner world of the great thinkers, and accordingly, you can expand and develop your own mind and knowledge.

Reading can, for a pleasant while, take you away from normality. Reading a fiction book gives you a chance to enter a fantasy, suspense, and curiosity domain just by engaging your attention. Reading self-help books can enrich your mind with advice, solutions, direction, inspiration, etc. It will expand your awareness and knowledge; each book or article will make you wiser and more intelligent.

Life becomes so much more interesting when you explore new avenues or venture into somebody else's imagination and creativity. Because books are small and compact, you can take a book with you anywhere you go, and they need no power supply, no charging of the battery, no interruption in between unless you do.

Reading is one of the cheapest forms of entertainment. It can stimulate your analytical thinking abilities and skills. It is even freely available on the internet or in libraries.

Reading Stimulates Creativity

Not many people have achieved success without knowledge and learning; the best way to absorb and acquire knowledge is through reading. One of the most powerful, yet probably underestimated personal development tools, is reading.

The benefits of reading are limitless, and it is an age-old tradition and pastime that will never become outdated. However, with the technological revolution forever gathering pace, many people now overlook the many health and therapeutic benefits of reading. Reading takes you to the world of imagination and enhances your creativity. It helps you explore life from different perspectives, building new and creative thoughts, images, and opinions in your mind. Reading makes you think creatively, fantasize, and use your imagination.

Many people like to grab a book, find a cozy corner, and forget all their cares and worries for a while as they experience and enjoy the peace and tranquillity gained by switching off and forgetting about the rest of the world. You can never be alone if you are reading.

Words describing scenes can never be entertaining if you cannot imagine what they are trying to depict. To truly enjoy a book, your mind is forced to imagine the scenes, and a compelling book is capable enough to turn your imagination into a movie of sorts, running just for you, in your mind.

Our brains are not wired to work in a particular way. We make it happen through our actions. Reading fiction books stimulates our creative thinking. We come up with different scenarios, alternate endings, and our own interpretations, which slowly improves our creativity.

Another one of the many reasons why reading is important is that it allows for creative thinking. Reading can inspire you when you are feeling bored, down, or in a rut. It can help give you that much-needed pick-me-up without having to search too far for it. Reading helps get the creative side of your brain thinking, unlike television, which does not use much creative brainpower.

Successful people read with the purpose of improving their understanding of the world. Creativity requires fuel, and that fuel includes gaining knowledge through reading and studying new things. The best innovators are the biggest learners and are not limited to the fields directly related to their work. They are the first readers; they know they can't maintain the leading edge while waiting for inspiration to strike. Reading stimulates imagination, which leads to the development of correlation, which further develops creativity. It does not stop here; it then develops problem-solving skills.

So, for every book, look for one main idea that you find new, useful, or challenges your existing beliefs. For example, when we see a movie, we can describe the main plot after months, but we don't care to register the paint color of the hero's office. If you try to remember the whole book, it will take away the joy. You need to learn "one big thing" from each book, and you will be on your way to success.

It is true that reading can improve creativity. Reading exposes you to new ideas, perspectives, and ways of thinking, which can help stimulate your imagination and expand your mind. Reading also helps improve your vocabulary, making it easier for you to express your thoughts and ideas more effectively.

Additionally, reading can help you develop empathy and understanding of others, as well as provide you with insights into different cultures and lifestyles. This exposure can help you bring a more diverse range of perspectives to your creative work, leading to more innovative and unique solutions.

However, it's worth noting that while reading can help improve creativity, it's just one aspect of the creative process. To truly unleash your creative potential, it's important to actively engage in creative activities, experiment, and take risks. Reading can be a valuable tool for supporting and enhancing your creativity, but it should be just one piece of the puzzle.

When Creativity Fails

"The only real mistake is the one from which we learn nothing." - Henry Ford

A little boy was just starting his school, and he was so excited to go to school and meet his teachers and new friends. On the very first day of school, one of the first things the teacher told them was, "Children, you are going to draw a picture." The boy was so excited because he loved to draw, so he immediately took his drawing book and started drawing. But the teacher said, "Wait, we are going to draw a picture of a flower." The little boy thought that it was okay because he loved flowers and he could draw all kinds of flowers, so he started drawing a flower. But the teacher said, "Wait, today we are going to draw a red flower with a green stem." The boy looked at the paper, but he had to follow what the teacher said, so he drew a red flower with a green stem. The next day, the teacher asked him to draw a picture of the animal kingdom. He was very excited, but the teacher said, "Wait, we are going to draw a picture of a bird." The little boy thought that it was okay because he loved birds and he could draw all different kinds of birds, so he started drawing a bird. But the teacher said, "Wait, today we are going to draw a white duck." Soon, he learned to wait for the exact instructions of the teacher, and he started doing what the teacher wanted him to do. But a change happened in the boy's life; he needed to shift to another school. On the very first day there, he was asked to draw a picture. While all the other boys started drawing on their own, this boy waited with his paper. The teacher asked him why he was not drawing, and the boy asked, "Ma'am, what picture should I draw?" "Anything you want, my boy," the teacher said. "Ma'am, which color?" the boy asked again. The teacher said, "Whatever color you prefer, my boy." Surprisingly, the boy drew a picture of a red flower with a green stem.

Ronak first started playing chess when he was 7 years old, and he always enjoyed puzzles and brain games. Growing up, he was interested in topics related to creativity, such as lateral thinking, cognitive bias, design thinking, etc. He also practiced Root Cause Analysis and managed to sort out critical business problems on various occasions. He needs to check out the latest in problem-solving, acquire some new techniques, and keep an open mind and not rule out any suggestions in order to come up with a solution that could turn the tables.

Creativity needs time, grit, and intentional effort. It takes time and practice to train the mind to think outside of the box – and that requires grit. The more passionate and perseverant we are, the more likely we are to succeed. Success also relies on top management's willingness to support employees' ideas and readiness to take risks. But the truth of the matter is that we've been trained for years to be systematic, to work tirelessly through procedures, and to be governed by policies. We've become tamed, in other words, and are thus afraid to break patterns and leave our comfort zones.

We can all be creative and innovative, but that doesn't happen overnight. "It wasn't raining when Noah built the ark," as Howard Ruff says. Small, incremental changes eventually add up and take shape. We may not need game-changing ideas, as minor improvements can really have a significant impact and might even turn the tables. Our opinion matters, and so we shouldn't be afraid to share it.

Creativity is interconnected with other personal development traits, such as habits, self-discipline, persistence, perseverance, etc. Creativity fails when we fail to be consistent in all of the above personal development elements. Failing in creativity means we get stuck in our present condition and may become out of competition in a short time.

At the time, Coca-Cola was facing increased competition from its rival, PepsiCo, and was losing market share. In an effort to regain market share, Coca-Cola decided to change the formula for its signature drink. The company spent millions of dollars developing a new formula and conducting taste tests to ensure that it would be well-received by consumers.

In April 1985, Coca-Cola launched "New Coke" to much fanfare. However, the response from consumers was overwhelmingly negative. People protested the change, and Coca-Cola was flooded with letters and calls from angry customers. Within three months, Coca-Cola was forced to bring back the original formula, which it rebranded as "Coca-Cola Classic."

The failure of "New Coke" was a major blow to Coca-Cola, and the company lost millions of dollars in the process. However, the experience taught the company a valuable lesson about the risks of changing a beloved product.

This story reminds us that even the most creative and innovative ideas can sometimes fail. However, it is important to learn from our failures and use them as an opportunity for growth and improvement. In the case of Coca-Cola, the failure of "New Coke" led the company to appreciate the value of its original formula and the importance of listening to its customers.

Conquer the creative block

Neelu was known for her beautiful paintings and had won many awards for her work. She was proud of her creativity and loved to express herself through her art.

One day, Neelu found herself facing a creative block. No matter what she tried, she couldn't seem to come up with any new ideas. She was frustrated and felt like a failure. She started to question her abilities as an artist and wondered if she would ever be able to paint again.

Feeling lost, Neelu decided to take a walk in the forest to clear her mind. As she was walking, she came across a wise old owl who asked her what was wrong. Neelu explained her situation, and the owl told her, "Creativity is like a river, sometimes it flows smoothly, and other times it gets blocked. But if you wait patiently, the water will find its way back."

The owl's words gave Neelu hope, and she realized that her creative block was just temporary. She decided to give herself time and space to recharge and not force herself to create. She took up new hobbies, read books, and explored new places.

With time, Neelu's creativity started to flow again. She was able to come up with new ideas and paint beautiful pictures once more. She learned that creativity is not always a steady stream and that it's okay to take a break and recharge.

So when creativity fails, it's important to give ourselves time and space to recharge. We should not force ourselves to create, but instead, allow ourselves to explore new things and find inspiration in the world around us. By taking care of ourselves and being patient, we can find our way back to our creativity and continue to create beautiful works of art.

Historical Failures due to Lack of Creativity

"Failure is not a lack of success, it's a lack of imagination." - Seth Godin

Throughout history, many instances of hindrances to creativity have led to significant failures. One example is the failure of Kodak, an iconic American photography company, to innovate and adapt to the digital age. Kodak was a dominant force in the photography industry for most of the 20th century, known for their film cameras and other photographic products. However, when digital photography began to gain popularity in the 1990s, Kodak failed to recognize its potential and instead focused on preserving its existing business model. Kodak was slow to develop digital cameras, and when they did release them, they were not as advanced as their competitors. Additionally, they failed to capitalize on the potential of digital storage and sharing, which became increasingly popular with the rise of the internet. As a result of this failure to innovate, Kodak's profits declined, and the company eventually filed for bankruptcy in 2012.

Similarly, there were other companies that failed to adapt to new technologies or consumer preferences leading to their downfall. For example, Blockbuster Video, once a household name in the video rental industry, failed to adapt to the rise of streaming services and digital downloads and eventually filed for bankruptcy in 2010. Nokia, a dominant force in the mobile phone industry in the early 2000s, failed to keep up with the smartphone revolution and the rise of Apple's iPhone. Sears, once the largest retailer in the United States, failed to adapt to the changing retail landscape. MySpace, once the largest social networking site, failed to keep up with the rise of Facebook. Borders, once the second-largest bookstore chain in the United States, failed to keep up with the shift to digital books. Pan Am, once the leading airline in the world, failed to adapt to the changing airline industry. Betamax, a video cassette format introduced by Sony in the 1970s, failed to gain widespread adoption due to its lack of flexibility. Edsel, a brand of cars introduced by Ford in the late 1950s, failed to resonate with consumers. The DeLorean Motor Company, which aimed to produce a sports car that would revolutionize the industry, was bankrupt by 1982. Google Glass, a wearable technology product introduced in 2013, failed to gain widespread acceptance due to concerns about privacy and the high cost, and it was discontinued in 2015. Sears Canada, a subsidiary of Sears Holdings, which operated department stores in Canada, declared bankruptcy in 2017 due to its failure to keep up with changing consumer trends.

These examples illustrate the importance of embracing creativity and innovation to remain competitive and relevant in a rapidly changing world. Companies must recognize the potential of new technologies and consumer preferences and adapt their business models accordingly to avoid becoming obsolete.

Obstacles to creative thinking

"The comfort zone is the great enemy to creativity; moving beyond it necessitates intuition, which in turn configures new perspectives and conquers fears."
- Dan Stevens

Creativity is an essential part of human experience that enables us to generate innovative ideas, solve problems, and create new things. However, there are many obstacles that can hinder our ability to be creative and limit our potential to come up with new and innovative ideas. These obstacles can be external or internal and can manifest in various ways, including fear of failure, lack of time, self-doubt, lack of inspiration, distractions, and pressure to conform. Identifying and addressing obstacles to creativity is essential for personal and professional growth, as well as for the development of society as a whole.

Several obstacles can hinder creativity, including:

• *Fear of failure:* One of the biggest obstacles in creative thinking is the fear of failure. When people are afraid to fail, they may avoid taking risks and trying new things that could potentially lead to innovative ideas. An aspiring writer who wants to publish a novel may struggle to start writing because of the fear of rejection or criticism from publishers and readers. To overcome this, it's important to embrace the idea of failure and understand that it's a necessary part of the creative process.

• *Distractions:* In our digital age, there are countless distractions that can take our attention away from creative activities, such as social media or constant notifications. These distractions can make it difficult to focus and engage in deep, creative work. To overcome this obstacle, it's essential to establish a conducive environment that minimizes distractions and fosters creativity.

• *Overthinking:* Overthinking a problem can lead to analysis paralysis and prevent the flow of creative thoughts. Overthinking can lead to excessive self-criticism, doubt, and a lack of confidence in one's abilities. To overcome this obstacle, it's essential to cultivate a mindset of experimentation and risk-taking. By focusing on the act of creation itself, rather than the outcome, one can free themselves from the constraints of overthinking and tap into their full creative potential.

• *Mental blocks:* Mental blocks, such as writer's block, can make it difficult to generate new ideas or express them effectively. To overcome mental blocks, it's essential to step back and approach the problem from a new perspective.

Additionally, incorporating mindfulness practices such as meditation and journaling can help to clear the mind and foster a sense of calm and clarity.

• *Stress and anxiety:* High levels of stress and anxiety can impact the ability to think creatively and make it difficult to focus on the task at hand. To overcome these obstacles, it's essential to prioritize self-care practices such as exercise, meditation, and adequate sleep. Additionally, creating a supportive environment and seeking out social support can help to alleviate stress and anxiety.

• *Conformity and pressure to conform:* In some environments, there may be pressure to conform to certain standards or ideas, which can stifle creativity and limit the exploration of new and unconventional ideas.

• *Lack of time:* Creativity requires time to explore ideas and experiment. When people are busy with daily tasks and obligations, they may not have the time or space to engage in creative activities.

• *Lack of inspiration:* Creativity is often sparked by inspiration, and when people lack inspiration or motivation, they may find it challenging to come up with new ideas. To overcome this obstaclc, seeking out inspiration from different sources or taking a break to recharge may be helpful.

• *Self-doubt:* Negative self-talk and self-doubt can hinder creativity. When people doubt their abilities, they may lack the confidence to take risks and explore new ideas. A designer who thinks their work isn't good enough may hesitate to share their ideas and miss out on valuable feedback and collaboration opportunities.

• *Lack of resources:* Creativity often requires resources like materials, equipment, or a supportive environment. When people lack these resources, they may find it challenging to be creative. An inventor with an innovative product idea may struggle to bring it to life due to a lack of funding, technology, or materials.

Overcoming these obstacles often requires a willingness to embrace uncertainty, try new things, and approach problems with a fresh perspective. By using these practical methods, you can overcome obstacles in creative thinking and find new and innovative solutions to the problems you face. Remember, the key is to keep an open mind and be willing to try new and different approaches.

Conclusion

In conclusion, creativity is not an innate gift reserved for a select few. Rather, it is a skill that can be developed and nurtured over time. It is a way of thinking that can be learned, practiced, and applied in various contexts. By igniting your creativity, you can unlock your full potential and achieve your aspirations.

"Spark Your Creativity" is a book that can significantly help anyone struggling with creativity. The book is written in an easily understandable and accessible manner for a broad audience. It provides practical advice and actionable tips for overcoming mental blocks and cultivating a more creative approach to problem-solving. The book also emphasizes the importance of habits in nurturing creativity and encourages readers to develop a consistent routine and a supportive environment that fosters creativity. Additionally, the book provides inspiring examples of successful creative individuals and their habits.

But sparking your creativity is not just about acquiring new skills and knowledge. It is also about changing your mindset and embracing a new way of thinking. It involves cultivating a sense of wonder and curiosity, seeing the world with fresh eyes, believing in your own abilities, and having the confidence to take risks and try new things.

By sparking your creativity, you can discover new passions, solve problems in innovative ways, and make a difference in the world. Creativity is a key ingredient in success, whether you are an artist, writer, professional, entrepreneur, or scientist. It sets you apart from others and enables you to stand out in a competitive marketplace.

As you finish reading this book, it is recommended to take action and apply what you have learned. Set aside time each day to engage in creative activities and never stop learning and growing. Honing your skills to recognize patterns and find solutions shifts your perspective and offers a new vantage point for exploration. Not only can creative thinking improve your performance at work, but it can also enhance every aspect of your life. Breaking away from your regular routine and trying something new is the key to fostering creative thinking in your daily life.

Remember, creativity is a lifelong pursuit that requires patience, persistence, and dedication. However, the rewards are immense. By sparking your creativity, you can transform your life, career, and world. You have the power to create something unique and meaningful. So, start today and spark your creativity!

Gratitude

This book is dedicated to my beloved parents whose continuous support and blessings helped me write another book on success.